THE SIGN OF THE BEAVER

by
Elizabeth George Speare

Teacher Guide

Written by
Anne Troy

Note

The Dell Yearling paperback edition of the book was used to prepare this teacher guide. The page references may differ in the hardcover or other paperback editions.

Please note: Please assess the appropriateness of this book for the age level and maturity of your students prior to reading and discussing it with your class.

ISBN 1-56137-242-0

To order, contact your local school
supply store, or—

Table of Contents

Chapters contain: Vocabulary Words and
Activities, Discussion Questions and
Activities, Supplementary Activities,
Predictions

Skills and Strategies

Thinking
Brainstorming, classifying
and categorizing, comparing
and contrasting, evaluating,
analyzing details

Literary Elements
Character, setting, plot
development, story map,
figurative language, conflict

Vocabulary
Synonyms/antonyms,
context clues

Comprehension
Predicting, sequencing,
cause/effect, inference,
compare information from
more than one source

Writing
Reports, journal, summary,
chapter titles, comparison/
contrast, narrative

Listening/Speaking
Participation in discussion,
presentation of reports

Summary

In the summer of 1769, twelve-year-old Matt is left to guard the cabin in the Maine wilderness while his father journeys to Massachusetts to bring the rest of the family to the new homestead. A series of disasters puts Matt in serious trouble—so serious that his survival is in doubt. He is rescued by Saknis, chief of the Beaver Indian tribe. Matt is taught survival skills by the Indians. Saknis, realizing that more and more white men will come, wants his grandson, Attean, to learn survival skills, too—he wants Attean to learn to read the white man's writing. If Matt will teach Attean to read, then the Indian boy will bring him food and game each day.

The boys are not comfortable with the bargain or with each other. They resent the position that Saknis has put them in, but slowly they learn to respect each other and to become friends.

Prereading Activity

This novel is a historical fiction book. What does this mean?

   (a) Historical — The characters of the story may be people who actually lived during the story's time period or be fictitious individuals.

      The setting of the story will be a previous time period. It is important that the customs and ideals of characters and events of history are accurate in relation to the historical setting.

   (b) Fiction — A story invented by the writer.

   (c) Historical Fiction may be based on real events, but includes made-up characters and experiences.

Initiating Activities

1. How long have your parents left you alone at home? a day? overnight? What did you like about it? How did you feel?

2. Have you ever gone camping? What did you need to survive?

3. Brainstorm the word "survival." The teacher will put the sketch on the following page on the board or large sheet of paper and record student responses. Students will relate survival to their camping experiences, then later they will use these same points for Matt's survival.

4. Draw a map of the New England states. Label each of the six states. Locate and label the following cities: Boston, Quincy, Portsmouth, and Bangor. Label the following bodies of water: Atlantic Ocean, Penobscot Bay, Penobscot River, Mattawamkeag River, and Piscataquis River. Also color and label Canada.

5. Use the map to show the location of Maine and Quincy, Massachusetts. How many miles is it, approximately? How long would it take us to travel by airplane? by car? by horse? by foot?

6. Look up Maine in the encyclopedia to find information about Maine's climate. What are the average temperatures and yearly rainfall? How does this compare to your state's climate?

Prediction
What do you think the title of the book means? (Teacher lists class responses on a large sheet of paper which may be kept in view until the answer is discovered in the book.)

Recommended Procedure
This book may be used in several ways: a) read to the entire class; b) read with the class; c) read in reading groups; d) read by an individual.

This book may be read one chapter at a time using the DRTA, Directed Reading Thinking Activity, Method. This technique involves reading a section, and then predicting what will happen next by making good guesses based on what has already occurred in the story. The predictions are recorded and verified after the subsequent reading has taken place. (See pages 6-7 of this guide.)

The Discussion Questions and Activities at the end of each chapter, as well as any supplementary activities are provided so that you may, using discretion, make selections from them that will be suitable for use by the children in your group.

You may wish to have students show knowledge of words in the vocabulary before reading the chapter by writing simple definitions in their own words. After reading, the students may need to redefine the words by referring to the text and/or a dictionary.

Survival Chart

How does Matt survive in the wild? What need does he have to have met in order to survive? Complete the chart below.

Needs	How He Gets Them
Food	
Water	
Warmth	
Shelter	
Love	
Companionship	
Mental Stimulation	

Using Predictions

We all make predictions as we read—little guesses about what will happen next, how a conflict will be resolved, which details will be important to the plot, which details will help fill in our sense of a character. Students should be encouraged to predict, to make sensible guesses as they read the novel.

As students work on their predictions, these discussion questions can be used to guide them: What are some of the ways to predict? What is the process of a sophisticated reader's thinking and predicting? What clues does an author give to help us make predictions? Why are some predictions more likely to be accurate than others?

Create a chart for recording predictions. This could be either an individual or class activity. As each subsequent chapter is discussed, students can review and correct their previous predictions about plot and characters as necessary.

Use the facts and ideas the author gives.

Use your own prior knowledge.

Apply any new information (i.e., from class discussion) that may cause you to change your mind.

Predictions

_____

_____

_____

_____

Prediction Chart

What characters have we met so far?	What is the conflict in the story?	What are your predictions?	Why did you make those predictions?

Graphic Organizers

Included in this guide are several types of graphic organizers, such as the Venn diagram, the T-diagram, and brainstorming or cluster circles. A variety of possible answers should be listed by the teacher either on large sheets of paper or the chalkboard. Only then should the students be asked to develop their own graphics. Students are encouraged to express their opinions, and to state what they know about a topic. The teacher lists these opinions and "facts" and later, as the children read and discover that some of their ideas are incorrect, these ideas may be crossed out on the sheets or board. Students should be encouraged to elaborate on their answers, justify their opinions, prove their predictions, and relate what they have read to their own lives.

T-diagrams show likenesses and differences of two characters, plots, settings, etc.

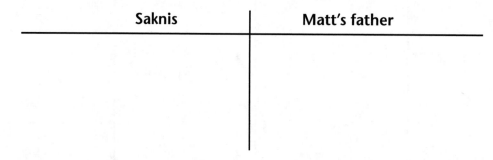

Venn diagrams are taken from math. Characteristics of two characters are listed, and the overlap or similarity may be seen.

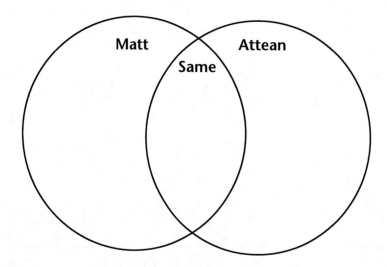

Chapter 1 — Pages 1-6

Vocabulary

fetch 2	puncheon 3	daubed 3	blunderbuss 4
mite 5	ruefully 5		

Vocabulary Activity

Ask the class to see if they can figure out the meaning of each underlined word by reading the following sentences. Discuss their responses and the true definitions. Find these words on the pages listed in the novel. This may be used as a pre- or post-reading activity.

1. The man made the puncheon table with a broad piece of wood having one flat side.
2. The child daubed the peanut butter on the bread.
3. The boy tried to teach the dog to fetch the newspaper.
4. A blunderbuss is not used by hunters today.
5. Grandpa says that fishing is a mite better in the big pond.
6. Ruefully, I admitted I'd made a mistake spending my allowance.

Discussion Questions and Activities

1. Story Map: Many stories have the same parts—a setting, a problem, a goal, and a series of events that lead to an ending or conclusion. These story elements may be placed on a story map. Just as a road map leads a driver from one place to another, so too a story map leads a reader from one point to another. There are many different types of story maps. Students may use the one included or make up their own. (See page 10 of this guide.)

   Read only page 1. What information do we have to begin a story map?

   - What is the setting?
   - Who is the main character?
   - What is the problem?

   As the story is read, more characters are added, and the setting and the problem (especially in this story) may be changed.

2. Begin an attribute web for Matt. (See pages 11-12 of this guide.)

Story Map

Characters_____

_____

Setting

Time and Place_____

_____

Problem

Problem_____

_____

_____

Goal

Goal_____

_____

_____

Beginning ⟶ Development ⟶ Outcome

Episodes

_____

_____

_____

_____

Resolution

Resolution_____

_____

_____

_____

Using Character Webs

Attribute webs are simply a visual representation of a character from the novel. They provide a systematic way for students to organize and recap the information they have about a particular character. Attribute webs may be used after reading the novel to recapitulate information about a particular character, or completed gradually as information unfolds. They may be completed individually or as a group project.

One type of character attribute web uses these divisions:

- How a character acts and feels. (How does the character act? How do you think the character feels? How would you feel if this happened to you?)

- How a character looks. (Close your eyes and picture the character. Describe him/her to me.)

- Where a character lives. (Where and when does the character live?)

- How others feel about the character. (How does another specific character feel about our character?)

In group discussion about the characters described in student attribute webs, the teacher can ask for backup proof from the novel. Inferential thinking can be included in the discussion.

Attribute webs need not be confined to characters. They may also be used to organize information about a concept, object, or place.

Attribute webs are a kind of semantic mapping. Students can move on from attribute webs to other creative kinds of mapping. They can be encouraged to modify attribute webs, use subdivisions, in whatever ways are useful to them personally. It is important to emphasize, especially to older children, that attribute webs are just a visual way to remember concepts. They provide the students with a tool to remember.

Attribute Web

The attribute web below will help you gather clues the author provides about a character in the novel. Fill in the blanks with words and phrases which tell how the character acts and looks, as well as what the character says and what others say about him or her.

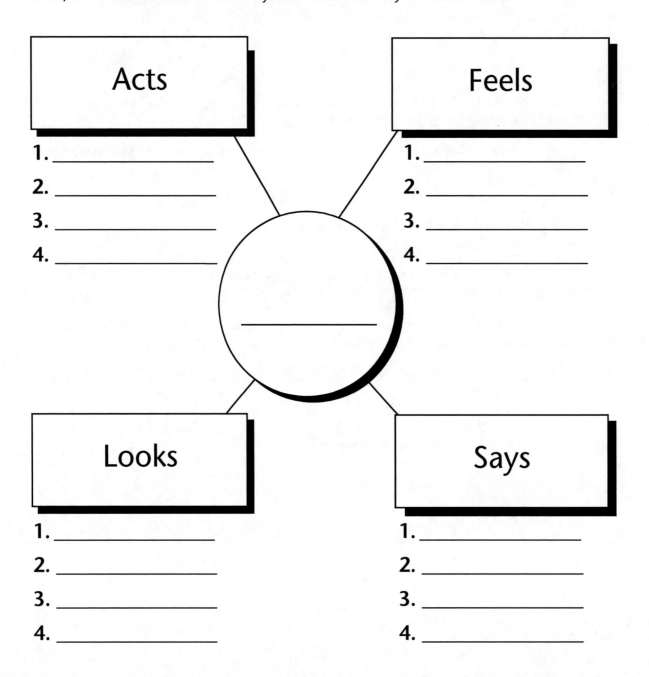

Acts

1. _____
2. _____
3. _____
4. _____

Feels

1. _____
2. _____
3. _____
4. _____

Looks

1. _____
2. _____
3. _____
4. _____

Says

1. _____
2. _____
3. _____
4. _____

3. Begin a time line.

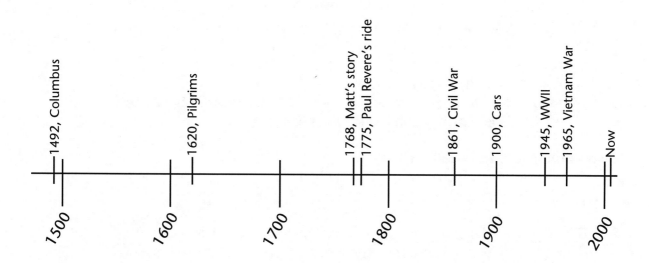

4. Why was Matt's father leaving him alone? Why couldn't he go with his father? Was Matt's father right to leave Matt in the wilderness? Why or why not?

5. Did children grow up faster in those days? Why?

Prediction
What do you think could happen to a twelve-year-old boy left on his own for seven weeks in the wilderness?

Group Research Activity
Divide the class into cooperative groups for research and making charts on each of the following topics: *trees, plants, animals, birds* and *insects, pioneer food, Indians, Indian values,* and *white man's values.* After each chapter is read, each group will add to their chart any new information learned from reading the novel or their outside reading. The charts will be displayed on the bulletin boards throughout reading of the novel.

Chapter 2 — Pages 7-10

Vocabulary

chinking 7	coaxed 8	blazed 9	proprietors 9
stock 9	hemlock 10		

© Novel Units, Inc.

13

Vocabulary Activity

Instruct the class to read the sentences below and then write the meaning for each italicized word without using a dictionary. Discuss the responses.

1. White men build the house; women *chink* the cracks.
2. The boy *coaxed* the fire with dry leaves.
3. He *blazed* a trail in the forest.
4. The *proprietors* of the store put out new ads.
5. My grandmother took great *stock* in the use of Vicks Vapor Rub for chest colds.
6. *Hemlock* trees were planted on the north and west sides of the house.

Discussion Questions and Activities

1. What was something that worried Matt? (Page 9, "...he just didn't like the feeling he had sometimes that someone was watching him.")

2. How do you think most settlers felt about the Indians? (page 9) What other information have you read about encounters between Indians and settlers?

3. Why wasn't Matt afraid of the Indians? (Page 9, "Most of 'em have left for Canada. The ones who stayed don't want to make any trouble.")

4. If you were living alone now, what are some of the things you might worry about?

5. Matt's father gave him some good advice on how to treat the Indians. What was it? (Page 9, "...Indians take great stock in politeness. Should you meet one, speak to him just the same as to the minister back home.") Why do you think this was good advice?

6. Why did Matt need a gun? (Page 8, "He depended on his gun to keep his stomach filled.") What does that mean?

7. In modern times what would happen to a twelve-year-old boy left by himself for seven weeks? Make a T-comparison chart.

Boy in 1768	Boy today

Prediction
How does the author hint that there will be trouble in the next chapter? Support your answer. Who do you think Matt's unexpected visitor might be?

Fire-Starting Demonstration
How do you start a fire with a flint? Find a scout leader or other qualified adult to demonstrate this skill.

Research Activity
Research one or all of these topics:
- The French and Indian War
- Jesuit priests as explorers
- Jesuit priests and the French and Indian War

Writing Activity
Begin writing a journal like Matt might have kept.

Chapter 3 — Pages 11-18

Vocabulary

pewter 13	singlehandedly 16	expedition 16	begrudging 17
hunch 18	burly 18	rage 18	

Vocabulary Activity
Direct the students to place an "S" on the line between the words if they believe the words have a similar meaning. If they think that the words have opposite meanings, instruct them to write "O" in the space.

pewter	S	metal
singlehandedly	S	unaided
expedition	S	journey
begrudgingly	O	willingly
hunch	S	guess
rage	O	calm
burly	O	slight

Discussion Questions and Activities
1. How would you feel if a stranger came into your house when your parents were away? Why did Ben's appearance worry Matt? (page 17)

2. What warnings that Ben was going to make trouble does the author give us? (Page 12, "...eyes that glittered in the weather-hardened face"; page 13, "His eye fell on the rifle..."; page 14, "I'm keeping as fur off from the river's I can, till things quiet down.")

3. Why was the loss of the gun so serious? (page 18, no protection, no way to get meat)

4. Matt had a hunch that warned him about Ben. Make an attribute web for Ben. There are many signs that tell us about the character.

5. What could Matt have done to have prevented Ben from taking the gun? (page 17)

6. What could have happened if Matt had awakened and caught Ben stealing the rifle?

7. Ben used colloquialisms. Some of the words and expressions were not grammatically correct. Make a list of Ben's expressions and the way we would say the same thing.

Prediction
How will Matt manage without a rifle for protection and for killing meat?

Writing Activity
What would Matt write in his journal about the lies he told Ben and about the loss of the gun?

Art Activities
1. Draw a picture of Matt's cabin surrounded by trees and the garden. (Refer to the author's description on pages 1-3.)

2. Draw a rifle, labeling the parts.

Chapter 4 — Pages 19-21

Vocabulary

deprived 19	nippy 19	shambles 20	wits 20
salvage 20			

Vocabulary Activity
Have students complete synonym chains for vocabulary words. For example:

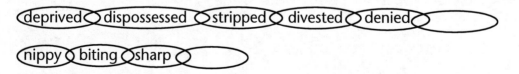

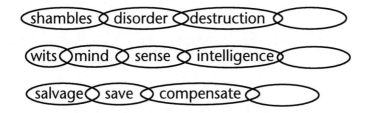

Discussion Questions and Activities

1. The author says that Matt "became a mite careless," page 19. What might have caused Matt to become careless? Do you agree or disagree with the author's statement? Support your answer.

2. Matt made two big mistakes that limited his food supply. What were they? (Pages 18 and 20, He went to sleep and Ben stole the gun; he had neglected to bar the door securely.) These two mistakes are different. Can you explain how they are different?

3. What did Matt need to do to keep things running smoothly? Brainstorm and make a schedule for Matt.

4. How might this chapter have ended if Matt had come back and surprised the bear?

5. What are the advantages a twelve year old has in living by himself? Would you like to try this for a week? for eight weeks? Why or why not?

Prediction
What will Matt have to do to make up for his mistakes?

Writing Activity
Brainstorm about the feelings that Matt is experiencing. Make a list of these feelings. Why do you think he is feeling this way? After the class brainstorming session, display the list of class responses. Students will use these feelings to write a diary entry expressing Matt's fear, anger, etc.

Chapter 5 — Pages 22-25

Vocabulary

endure 22	persuaded 22	bellowing 23	boggy 23
dazed 23	probing 24		

Vocabulary Activity
Match each word with its definition. Make a word puzzle with these words.

17

1. endure   tolerate; bear; suffer
2. persuade   urge; influence; convince
3. bellow   loud cry; roar; shout
4. boggy   swampy
5. daze   stun; bewilder
6. probe   investigate; search

Teacher Note: The words are across from their definitions. Mix them up when presenting them to students!

Discussion Questions and Activities
1. Read just page 22. What do you think will happen that will change everything for Matt? (Teacher lists class responses.)

2. What caused Matt's problem? (Page 22, "He was hungry for a bit of something tasty.")

3. Have you ever been stung by a bee? How do some people react to bee stings?

4. Do you think it was just chance or fate that the Indians were there when Matt needed them? Support your position.

5. Did the Indians act in surprising or unexpected ways? Why do you think that the Indians were so kind to Matt? (page 24)

6. The Indians seemed to know a lot about doctoring and medicines. What kind of medicine do you think they gave to Matt? How did the Indians know so much about medicine?

7. What might have happened to Matt if the Indians were not there?

Prediction
How will Matt repay the Indians for saving his life? Write the class predictions on the board. Evaluate the predictions. Arrange them in order of best ideas to worst.

Research Activity
How can honey be harvested safely? What would have been a better way for Matt to have tried to get the honey? Interview a beekeeper. Find information in the library and encyclopedia. Prepare a class report or bulletin board.

Chapter 6 — Pages 26-31

Vocabulary

resentful 27	abruptly 27	hobbled 27	pesky 28
incomprehensible 31	defiance 31	stalked 31	

Vocabulary Activity

Use each of the vocabulary words in a sentence. Share your sentences with a classmate.

Discussion Questions and Activities

1. Why didn't Matt realize his ankle was sprained?

2. Why do you think Matt told the Indian the truth about his father? Remember he didn't tell Ben the truth.

3. We learn about characters in a story by:

   - what the author tells us
   - what the character says and does
   - what others say about the character

What words are used to describe Attean? Ask the students to find words and phrases on pages 28-31. The teacher will list the words on the attribute web which will be used in future activities.

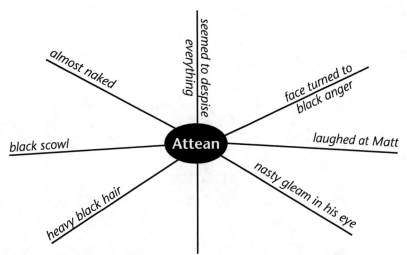

4. Why was the gift of a book important to the Indian?

5. How had the white men fooled the Indians? (page 31)

6. What does the word "treaty" mean? The teacher will ask the students for the first word that they think of when they hear the word "treaty" and will record their responses.

7. What did Saknis mean when he used the word "treaty"? (page 30, an agreement to bring birds and rabbits to Matt if Matt will teach Attean to read)

8. Why do you think Attean did not like Matt?

Prediction
Do you think Attean and Matt will become friends? Why or why not?

Writing Activity
Do you think the gift of the book *Robinson Crusoe* was a good gift for Saknis? Why or why not? What favorite book that you have read would you have given to Saknis (if it had been written at that time)? Write a brief summary of your favorite book.

Art Activity
Read the descriptions of Attean and his grandfather on pages 26 and 28 of the book. Draw pictures of them.

Chapter 7 — Pages 32-35

Vocabulary

| heathen 32 | disdainfully 33 | rigid 33 | finicky 33 |
| impatience 34 | grudgingly 34 | | |

Vocabulary Activity
Have the students collaborate on making word maps. A sample map for "rigid" follows.

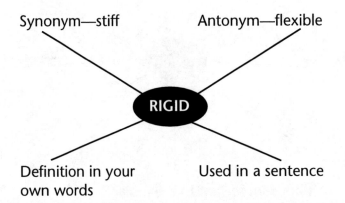

Display word maps as part of the bulletin board. Different colored markers may be used.

Discussion Questions and Activities

1. If you were Matt, how would you begin teaching someone to read? List class responses.

2. The first lesson did not go well. What letters or symbols would you have used with Attean?

3. Why do you think the Indian boy did not like to be close to Matt?

4. Why did Attean leave the cabin so suddenly? Have you ever felt like giving up on something because it takes too long to learn or do?

Prediction
Do you think Attean's leaving was the end of the lessons? Why or why not?

Writing and Art Activities

1. Write an ABC book for Attean using things he might know. Illustrate the book. Display ABC Books on a "Reading in Pioneer Times" bulletin board.

2. Titles of chapters are very important clues. Go back and write titles for each of the chapters read.

Chapter 8 — Pages 36-38

Vocabulary
scornfully 38   salvage 38   adz 38

Vocabulary Activity
Use each word in a sentence. Rewrite the sentence omitting the word. Ask a classmate to complete the sentence.

Discussion Questions and Activities

1. Do you think Matt's strategy of teaching Attean how to read by reading the book *Robinson Crusoe* was a good one? Why or why not?

2. If you were to use Matt's strategy for teaching how to read by reading a book, what book would you choose?

3. Why did Matt think Robinson Crusoe lived like a king? (Page 38, Matt and his father had come to Maine with only one axe and an adz.)

4. How do you feel about Attean's statement: "White man not smart like Indian. Indian not need thing from ship. Indian make all thing he need"? (page 38) How would you answer Attean?

5. How do you think Attean felt about the white men? Was he justified? Support your point of view.

Prediction
What do you think Matt will learn from Attean during the reading lessons?

Chapter 9 — Pages 39-44

Vocabulary

pouch 39	spliced 40	snare 40	nonchalantly 41
resigned 41	scorning 41	devised 41	contemptuous 41
mercilessly 42	stockstill 42		

Vocabulary Activity
Have students show knowledge of words before reading the chapter by writing simple definitions in their own words or good guesses of the meanings of the vocabulary words. Ask the students to read for verification or ask students to check their definitions in the dictionary.

Discussion Questions and Activities
1. Why do you think Attean continued to bring food to Matt after he had learned to snare animals?

2. How much of *Robinson Crusoe* do you think Attean understood? Prove your answer by finding a sentence to illustrate this in the chapter.

3. What do you think Attean meant when he said on page 43 that it would be better to die than to be a slave? Do you agree with his statement? Why or why not?

4. Matt had never questioned the wild man being Robinson Crusoe's slave until Attean was offended. Why was Matt troubled? (page 44)

5. What did Matt learn in this chapter? Did he learn something more important than the Indians' way of catching fish?

Prediction
Will Attean come back? Why or why not?

Group Chart Activity

Add to charts on trees, plants, animals, birds and insects, pioneer food, Indians, Indian values, and white man's values that was started in Chapter 1. What have you learned through this story? What would you like to learn?

Writing Activities

1. Which do you think was more important for Matt to do in teaching Attean to read—the letters and sounds or the reading of *Robinson Crusoe*? Support your opinion with proof from the story or from your own experience. Student responses will be included as part of a bulletin board, "Reading in Pioneer Times."

2. Matt had never thought much about slavery. Reread page 44. What would he have written in his journal?

3. What title would you give this chapter?

Art Activity

Reread pages 39-40. Draw a rabbit trap. Label the parts and write the directions under the pictures.

Chapter 10 — Pages 45-50

Vocabulary

suspicion 45	intently 46	impressive 47	resentment 50
scorn 50	pondering 50		

Vocabulary Activity

Take the vocabulary words for the last two chapters (or three or four). Play a 20 questions-type game (pairs, groups, or whole class). One student or the teacher selects a word for the class or group to identify by asking up to 20 questions (or 10 questions) about that word which may be answered by "yes," "no," or "sometimes."

Discussion Questions and Activities

1. Why do you think Matt "felt weak with relief" when Attean returned the next day? (page 45)

2. Why do you think Attean suggested that Matt go fishing? (page 47, to make him look ridiculous; to show him Indian fishing)

3. What did Matt learn from Attean? (page 49, to make a fish hook and to light a fire using a stone) Do you think you could do these two things when you camp?

4. Do you think Matt and Attean were becoming friends? Why or why not? Prove it. (page 50)

5. Should Matt have lied about Friday no longer being a slave to Robinson Crusoe? In what other ways might he have solved the problem? (pages 45-46) How would you have solved the problem?

6. Explain what Attean was doing that was more important than just bringing Matt food every day. (page 49) Why was this more important?

7. Explain the saying, "Give a man a fish, and you feed him for a day. Teach a man to fish, and you feed him for a lifetime." (Unknown, *International Thesaurus of Quotations*, page 646)

8. Why did Attean talk to the fish? (Page 50, "I say to him not to tell other fish...Not scare away.")

Writing Activity
Write step-by-step directions on how to make something or how to do something.

Chapter 11 — Pages 51-58

Vocabulary

| misshapen 52 | wary 52 | disdainful 54 | puny 57 |
| disgruntled 58 | gingerly 58 | | |

Vocabulary Activity
Use the vocabulary words from the last three chapters in a Verbal Tennis game.

Line up pupils in two rows facing each other. The contestants take turns giving out words from the board. The first contestant on the opposite side gives a synonym of the given word, the next contestant on the first side gives another synonym, and so on, words being batted back and forth as long as the synonyms hold out. Phrases, as well as words, are used. The first side to run out of synonyms gets a point against it. The side producing the last synonym starts with the new word; it is given by the person who stands next to the last contestant to furnish a synonym.

Discussion Questions and Activities
1. Why did Attean continue to come for lessons? How did he make Matt feel uncomfortable and ridiculous? (Matt had to rethink things he had always believed, e.g., slavery, fishing, hunting, and woman's work.)

2. The author uses colloquial expressions in this book. How would you explain, "Attean thought a sight of that dog"? (page 54)

3. What do you think the author intended when he wrote about Matt "...he trusted Attean. He didn't really like him"? (page 54)

4. What is the author referring to in the title of the book? (Pages 55-56, The sign of the beaver belonged to Attean's family. They carved a crude figure of the beaver on the trees by the beavers' dams.)

5. Compare the way the Beaver tribe showed ownership of land with the way the white man today shows ownership of land and possessions. Use the Venn diagram to list class responses.

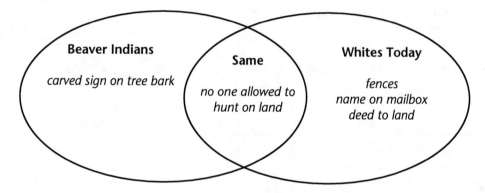

6. How were Attean and Matt like Robinson Crusoe and Friday? (page 57)

7. What did Matt want from Attean? (Attean's respect)

8. Compare the signs that Attean made to find his way in the forest to the ways that white men used. Which type of sign do you think was better? Why?

Prediction
How can Matt earn Attean's respect?

Research Activity
Make an oral or written report on beavers and beaver dams.

Art Activity
Reread page 52. Draw a picture of Attean's dog.

Writing Activity
If students have dogs of their own, they may write a comparison of their dogs and their feelings about them to Attean and his feelings about his dog.

Chapter 12 — Pages 59-62

Vocabulary
envious 59   stalking 59   chagrined 60   frayed 61
flimsy 61

Vocabulary Activity
Create a word search with vocabulary words for a classmate to decode.

Discussion Questions and Activities
1. How was the bow Attean and Matt made better than the one Matt made?

2. Make a list of things Matt learned from Attean. What do you think Attean learned from Matt?

Matt Learned	Attean Learned
chew sap from a spruce	
make a fish hook	
spear fish	
light fire with stone	
how to make medicine	

3. Matt noticed that Attean did not hunt for sport but only for food or something necessary. How do you feel about hunting wild animals for sport?

4. Why do you think Attean taught Matt to make bows and arrows rather than make them for him?

Art and Writing Activity
Reread pages 60-61. Write down the step-by-step directions for making a bow and arrow. Illustrate the steps.

Chapter 13 — Pages 63-67

Vocabulary

indignant 64	defiant 65	goaded 65	shrewdly 66
improvise 66	verily 67		

Vocabulary Activity
Ask students to look at each word and answer the following questions:
1) What is it?
2) What is it like?
3) What are some examples?

Discussion Questions and Activities
1. Why did Attean hate the iron trap?

2. If you were Matt would you have left the fox? Why or why not? What problems would Matt have had freeing the fox?

3. Do you agree or disagree with Attean that the white man's iron traps were bad? List arguments for using or not using them.

Iron Traps

Pro	Con
•More effective than Indian methods	•Cruel way to hunt •Does not always kill animal •Too many animals are killed

4. How do we know Attean was learning English even though he didn't want to learn it? (page 67)

Research Activity
What types of traps are used for capturing animals? Which are the most humane? Which cause the most suffering?

Art Activity
Draw pictures of the different types of animal traps.

Chapter 14 — Pages 68-70

Vocabulary
inspiration 68

Vocabulary Activity
Make a list of synonyms and antonyms for the vocabulary word.

Discussion Questions and Activities
1. Where did Matt get more stories for Attean? (page 68, the Bible)

2. What did Matt discover about Attean's people when he told him the story of Noah and the flood?

3. How do you think Attean learned the story of Noah?

Chapter 15 — Pages 71-75

Vocabulary

magnificent 71	grouse 71	immense 72	loomed 72
distracted 73	solemnness 74	resentful 75	

Vocabulary Activity
One student picks a vocabulary word and gives three meanings to the group. One meaning is false. The student who guesses the incorrect meaning gets a point and becomes the next leader.

Discussion Questions and Activities
1. How did Matt help Attean kill the bear? (Page 72, He threw his dead rabbit at the bear's head.) Do you think this was enough for Attean to consider Matt a hero? Was this a way for Matt to win respect?

2. Why did Attean talk to the dead bear? (Page 74, "I tell bear I do not want to kill...I ask bear to forgive that I must kill.")

3. Do you think Matt deserved equal credit for killing the bear? Why or why not?

4. What did Attean think was squaw work? Do you think certain jobs are for women and certain jobs are for men? List them. Why do you think this is true?

Men's Jobs	Women's Jobs

Prediction

What do you think Attean will tell the other Indians? Will he even tell them about Matt's role in killing the bear?

Writing Activities

1. Write Matt's diary entry for this day.

2. How does the author describe Matt's fear? (pages 72-73) Write about an incident when you were afraid.

Chapter 16 — Pages 76-83

Vocabulary

hideously 76	barred 78	wavering 78	pungent 78
array 78	dignity 79	boisterous 80	narrative 81
contortions 81			

Vocabulary Activity

Match each word with its definition.

1. hideous   twisted position or shape (9)
2. barred   stateliness and nobility (6)
3. waver   secured or obstructed by bars (2)
4. pungent   story (8)
5. array   extremely ugly (1)
6. dignity   noisy (7)
7. boisterous   adornment; dress (5)
8. narrative   keen; penetrating (4)
9. contortion   falter; sway (3)

Discussion Questions and Activities

1. Why was Matt worried? (Page 76, He wondered where his father was. Had he met with an accident or a bear?)

2. Why was Matt invited to the Indian feast? Do you think Attean gave him credit for the victory over the bear? Why or why not? Prove it.

3. What do you think was strange about the feast?

4. Why was Matt such an attraction at the feast?

5. How do you know Attean was a gifted storyteller? (pages 80-81, the audience's reaction)

6. Why didn't Attean eat the bear meat? (Page 82, "This my bear...I kill. Not eat. Maybe not get any more bear.") Explain this.

Prediction
Will Matt's father return? Why do you think this?

Art Activity
Draw scenes from the Indian celebration. (page 78)

Writing Activity
What would Matt remember most about the feast? Write how he would describe the feast in his diary.

Chapter 17 — Pages 84-89

Vocabulary

awesome 85	ramshackle 85	discarded 85	alternately 85
genial 86	taggle 86	wampum 87	lamely 87
bounty 88			

Vocabulary Activity
Make a crossword or any other type of puzzle using at least six of these vocabulary words.

Discussion Questions and Activities
1. Why did Attean's grandmother not want Matt to be at the feast? (Pages 87-88, White men had killed Attean's mother.)

Prediction
Will Matt ever visit the Indian village again? Why did he want to go back?

Art Activity
Draw the Indian village as described in this chapter.

Research Activity
Research the French and Indian War. Divide the class into two groups—the Indians and the white people. The groups are to research and collect evidence concerning their point of view. Debate: Why did the white men take the Indian land, kill the Indian people, kill the wildlife, etc.? Why did the Indians kill white men and burn their homes and crops? Each group will present their view.

Teacher Facts
French and Indian Wars (1689-1768)
There were a series of wars between Britain and France that went on almost without interruption. The Indian tribes of the Northeast were sympathetic to the French and fought with them against the British. The ultimate aim was domination of the Eastern part of the continent, capture of the seaboard towns, and capture of the western frontier forts and frontier settlements. To the American settlers, the fighting meant raids by either nation or even more horrible, the Indian border warfare. The last and most important American conflict was simply called the "French and Indian War" (1755).

Penobscot Indians
The Penobscots were part of the Wahanaki Nation. Wahanaki means "those living at the sunrise" or easterners. Penobscot means "rocky place" referring to the falls between Oldtown and Bangor, Maine—near Penobscot Bay and the Penobscot River. The tribe came from the southwest to Maine. They encountered French and English fishermen and explorers in the 16th century. They were visited by Champlain in 1604. The Penobscots assisted the French during the French and Indian Wars, but they made peace in 1749. They did not move with the rest of the Wahanaki Nation to Canada, but stayed in Maine where the principal settlement was in Oldtown Island. In present times they have a representative at sessions of the Maine state legislature. In 1768, at the time of our story, there were about seven hundred members of the Penobscot tribe.

Brainstorm how history might have been different; i.e., how the disagreements between the two groups could have been prevented. Students' responses are to be listed and used as part of the bulletin boards.

Chapter 18 — Pages 90-98

Vocabulary

detected 91	warily 91	ferociously 92	placid 93
frenzied 93	flaunting 93	substantial 94	gaunt 94
relenting 95	intricate 96		

Vocabulary Activity
Put the vocabulary words in alphabetical order. Arrange the words into sets of two words. Since there are ten words, there should be five sets of two words each. Use each set of two words in the same sentence.

Discussion Questions and Activities
1. Why do you think Matt tried to save Attean's dog?

   • because he could not stand to leave any animal in a trap
   • to help his friend

2. Why hadn't Attean told Matt about his sister? (Page 97, "Attean think squaw girl not good for much.")

3. How did Attean's grandmother show approval of Matt? (Page 96, She washed his wound and put medicine on it.)

4. Knowing how the Indian grandmother felt about white men, why do you think she took care of Matt?

5. Why do you think Attean pretended not to care for his dog? (page 98)

Prediction
Why do you think Matt's family had not returned?

Writing Activities
1. What would be a good title for this chapter? All members of the class will write a title. The class will vote on the best title.

2. Have you lost a pet or has your pet been injured? Write about your experience. Share your story with the class.

Chapter 19 — Pages 99-105

Vocabulary
forfeit 101   retorted 103   ordeal 104

Vocabulary Activity
Hangman Game: Using the vocabulary words which have been introduced so far in the book, think of a word and draw blanks to represent the number of letters in that word. Draw a noose on the board. (This may be a simple number 7 with a rope dangling

from it.) The child must guess which letters are in the word. When a child guesses a correct letter, fill it in its proper place. If a child guesses a wrong letter, draw one part of a stick figure under the noose until a whole body is completed. The parts which must be drawn on the figure are a head, a line for the body, arms, legs, hands, feet, eyes, nose, and mouth. If there are double letters in the word, both should be filled in when the letter is guessed. If the body is completed before the word is guessed, the teacher (or other leader) wins. If the word is guessed before the body is completed, the children are the winners. The child who guesses the word first may take the teacher's place.

Discussion Questions and Activities
1. What did Matt learn from the Indian women? Why was it important for Matt and all white men to learn to do women's work? (pages 99-100)

2. How did Matt win Attean's respect? (page 102)

3. What did we learn about Attean's grandmother? How is she like your grandmother? (Teacher will develop comparison by first using a T-diagram and then a Venn diagram.)

T-Diagram

My grandmother	Attean's grandmother
old	old
kind	kind
loves children	loves children
spoils me	likes her grandchild
comes to visit	

Venn Diagram

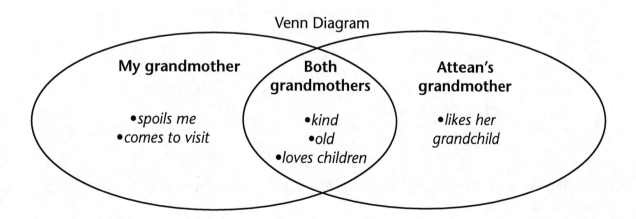

33

4. How are the games that the Indian boys played similar to games we play?

5. How did Matt prove himself at the Indian village? How did you or a new boy have to prove yourself/himself to your/his peers? Is this "proving yourself" true for girls, too? How do girls do it?

6. How did the Indian boys trick Matt? (Pages 101-103, He lost his shirt in a game.)

Prediction
If Matt's family does not come, will Matt "fit in" at the Indian village?

Writing Activities
1. What would Matt write in his journal about games with the Indians?

2. Make up directions for the games the Indians played. Try to play one of the games.

Chapter 20 — Pages 106-109

Vocabulary
    manitou 107

Vocabulary Activity
Look for this word in the dictionary. Find the pronunciation of this word and the definition.

Discussion Questions and Activities
1. Attean was afraid and sad as he went out to find his manitou. This is like an initiation into manhood. Are there any ceremonies somewhat like this for us? When does a boy become a man?

2. How did Attean prepare himself for his manitou? (page 108)

    *   had to learn many things
    *   bathe himself
    *   take a special medicine
    *   go into forest and build shelter
    *   fast from food
    *   pray and sing songs

3. If Attean found his manitou, he would return to his village with a new name. What would be a good name for Attean?

Writing Activity
What would each day be like for Attean? How would Attean feel as he searched for his manitou? Make up a day-by-day account of Attean's search for his manitou.

Chapter 21 — Pages 110-114

Vocabulary
reproach 110   unhampered 113   boisterous 114

Vocabulary Activity
Make a word map for each of the vocabulary words. (See sample map on page 20 of this guide.)

Discussion Questions and Activities
1. What great honor did Saknis offer Matt? (Page 112, "Saknis teach white boy hunt moose like Attean. White boy and Attean be like brother.")

2. Why was Matt "splitting logs with a fury" after Attean and his grandfather left? (Page 113, He wanted to go with them but he'd promised his father to watch the cabin.) What would you have done? What if Matt's father never returns?

3. Do you think Matt was foolish and stubborn in his decision to wait for his parents' return? Why or why not?

4. Why do you think Attean did not say good-bye?

Prediction
How do you think this book is going to end?

Chapter 22 — Pages 115-119

Discussion Questions and Activities
1. How had Matt finally gained Attean's respect? (page 115, "...by doing nothing, just by staying here and refusing to leave")

2. How would you explain to Attean the concept of buying land and owning land? Role play.

3. Attean gave Matt a special farewell present of his dog. What special farewell present would you give to your best friend?

4. Do you think it was more difficult for Attean to give Matt his dog or Matt to give Attean the watch?

Prediction
Do you think Matt will see Attean some time in the future?

Chapter 23 — Pages 120-126

Vocabulary
shucked 120	beseeching 121	ventured 122	enviously 122
prowess 122	intricately 123	feat 123	scant 124
trenchers 125	pesky 125		

Vocabulary Activity
In cooperative groups make bingo cards using the vocabulary words of several chapters. The caller of the game may use the vocabulary words or the word definitions. Make a caller answer card.

Discussion Questions and Activities
1. Matt stayed very busy. How did he prepare for winter?

2. Do you think Matt was lonely? Why or why not?

3. If you were alone in the woods like Matt, how would you stay busy?

4. Complete the Nature of Conflict Chart (page 37 of this guide) with the group.

Writing Activity
Choose one conflict in your life. Describe the conflict, identify the type, and describe how it was resolved.

Art Activity
Draw a picture of Matt in the new clothes he made for himself.

Chapter 24 — Pages 127-129

Vocabulary
knack 128	floundered 128

The Nature of Conflict

As is true in real life, the characters in novels face many conflicts. When two people or forces struggle over the same thing, conflicts occur. The excitement in novels develops from the use of the three main types of conflict: (1) person against person, (2) person against nature or society, and (3) person against him/herself.

Below, list some of the conflicts from the novel. In the space provided, briefly describe the conflict and indicate which type of conflict is involved, printing "PP" for person vs. person, "PN" for person vs. nature or society, and "PS" for person vs. self. Then choose three of the conflicts and describe how each was resolved.

Conflict	Description	Type

Conflict #1 resolution: _____

Conflict #2 resolution: _____

Conflict #3 resolution: _____

Vocabulary Activity

Write the words from several chapters on index cards, one word per card. Make enough sets so that students can work in small groups. One student chooses a card from a face-down pile without showing it to anyone else. The student then draws a picture representing the word, but may not say anything. The first student in the group to guess the word gets a point, and the student with the most points wins.

Discussion Questions and Activities

1. Why was Matt happy in a lonely cabin? (Page 129, He was no longer afraid of winter. Winter had come and since he now had snow shoes, he was not a prisoner in the cabin.)

2. What were the winter dangers for Matt? How do you think he will face them?

Prediction

There is one chapter left in the book. Will this story have a happy ending or a sad one? What do you think will happen? (Teacher lists all the possible endings on the board.)

Chapter 25 — Pages 130-135

Vocabulary

clamor 131	fend 133	jerky 134

Vocabulary Activity

The students will use vocabulary words from the chapter plus others of their choosing to make crossword puzzles on graph paper. The students will write a question for each word and develop an answer sheet. The teacher will check the answers and distribute the puzzles to other students.

Discussion Questions and Activities

1. What did Matt compare in his life to Attean's discovery of his manitou? (page 133, praise from his father for doing a man's job)

2. What do you think Matt's family will think was the best story Matt had to tell? Why?

Post-reading Questions

1. What did Matt learn?

2. How was the setting of the book important?

3. What was the author's message? What do you think is the most important thing to remember in the story?

4. What did you learn about Indians? What would you like to learn about Indians?

Post-reading Activities

Point of View
Divide the class into small groups. Each person in each group should tell the story from a different point of view.

Emotions
Ask each student to choose a character from the novel and write a list of feelings or emotions expressed by that character. All items on the list must start with the beginning initial of the character's name. When the students have finished their lists, have them share their choices with classmates, describing the circumstances in the story that led them to select those words.

Art Activities
1. There are no pictures in this book. What picture or symbol would you use for each character?

2. Paint a mural of the principal events in *The Sign of the Beaver*.

Readers' Theater
Divide the book into scenes and write, produce and present Readers' Theater scripts for other classes.

Social Studies Activity
Plan and prepare a pioneer meal. You might include corn bread, molasses, honey, stew, pumpkin, and cranberries.

Writing and Art Activity
Complete the Comparison Activity Sheet on the following page.

Comparison Activity Sheet

A **simile** uses the words "like" or "as" to compare two very different things.

A **metaphor** suggests a comparison by saying one thing is another without using "like" or "as."

Personification is used when a writer gives human characteristics to an animal or an object.

Find examples of similes, metaphors, and personification in this book. Then make up two examples of your own. Draw pictures of the figures of speech.

metaphor: sky   was   blaze

personification: stars   were   dancing

simile: stubborn   as a   mule